10

What's on your top 10 list?

This interactive journal is the inspiring

companion to the award-winning "10"

book, and is a perfect way to guide you

forward on your journey. It's all here:

inspiring prompts, thought-provoking

questions and—most importantly—lots

of space for you to create your most

meaningful lists. These lists will help you

to shape your life, to express your spirit,

to bring you joy and satisfaction, and to

create a life of fulfillment and adventure.

At any moment you can change everything. Your new and improved life can begin now. Just make a list of what's truly important to you. Start here and your life will never be the same again.

Written lists are tangible. They provide focus and direction, clarify who you are and what you love, reorder your priorities, and give you a glimpse of some of the exciting things to come.

Say yes to life and see where it leads you. "Yes" opens the door to endless possibilities. "No' may be safer, but you'll always regret the things you didn't do more than the things you did do.

SAY yes TO life.

_____

_____

_____

_____

_____

_____

_____

_____

_____

Where are you on your journey—and why are you where you are? Is it because you want to

_____

_____

_____

_____

_____

_____

_____

_____

_____

_____

_____

_____

be there—or because other people put you there? Be sure you're choosing your own path.

_____

_____

_____

_____

_____

_____

_____

_____

_____

Consider these questions: What's your philosophy of life? What's your personal mission?

_____

_____

_____

_____

_____

_____

_____

_____

_____

_____

_____

_____

_____

What's your obsession or grand intention? What's your personal motto or bumper sticker?

Possibilities first; practicality later. Give yourself permission to list big, wonderful, impractical ideas. You can always come back later and build the practicality into your possibilities.

What
is your
heart's
desire

Most limitations are self-imposed. As Michael Nolan stated, "It's not who we are that holds us back it's who we think we're not." Never let an artificial ceiling stop you from pursuing your dreams.

Forget your excuses. Records are set all the time by people who didn't have the right ability or background—or who didn't know any better. Can't usually means won't. You can if you will.

Reminders for an adventurous life: follow your dreams, indulge your curiosity, get off the beaten rack, welcome the unexpected, challenge the experts, ignore naysayers, be true to yourself.

be bo

be dar

be dif

ld.
ing
ferent.

Big goals equal big outcomes. Little goals equal little outcomes. No goals mean no outcomes or worse, someone else's). Decide what you want out of life. Don't let others decide for you.

_____

_____

_____

_____

_____

_____

_____

_____

_____

Give a name and a date to your goal and it suddenly becomes real. Instead of, "I want to raise

_____

_____

_____

_____

_____

_____

_____

_____

_____

_____

_____

_____

horses someday," try writing, "The gates to my Wild Stallion Ranch swing open on May 1st."

You don't need to know how you're actually going to achieve a goal when you set it. Just list all

_____

_____

_____

_____

_____

_____

_____

_____

the emotionally satisfying reasons why you want to achieve it—and the how will become clear.

_____

_____

_____

_____

_____

_____

_____

_____

_____

_____

_____

HOW INSPIRED ARE YOU?

HOW ARE YOU INSPIRED?

_____

_____

_____

_____

_____

_____

_____

_____

_____

What do you really want to do tomorrow? Next week? Next year? Make a list of what's stopping

_____

_____

_____

_____

_____

_____

_____

_____

_____

_____

_____

_____

you. Remember: Hurdles are for jumping. Problems are for solving. Obstacles can be overcome.

_____

_____

_____

_____

_____

_____

_____

_____

_____

_____

Two lists to write down every morning: 1. What are the three most important things for me to

_____

_____

_____

_____

_____

_____

_____

_____

_____

_____

_____

_____

_____

_____

_____

_____

_____

_____

_____

_____

_____

_____

accomplish today? 2. What are the distractions I'm *not* going to squander my time on today?

_____

_____

_____

_____

_____

_____

_____

_____

_____

_____

_____

_____

_____

_____

_____

_____

_____

_____

_____

_____

Did you make a *real* decision? Deciding something is one thing, but *doing* something is another

_____

_____

_____

_____

_____

_____

_____

_____

_____

_____

_____

_____

You can tell when you've made a real decision because there will be an action attached to it.

Where do you
draw the line
between
POSSIBLE &
IMPOSSIBLE?

Always know in your heart that you are far bigger than anything that can happen to you.

Setbacks are opportunities. Learn from them; use them to make you stronger and wiser.

_____

_____

_____

_____

_____

_____

_____

_____

_____

One of the greatest sources of energy is having pride in what you do. List the things you will

_____

_____

_____

_____

_____

_____

_____

_____

_____

_____

_____

_____

be most proud to accomplish in the years to come. For yourself. For your family. For the world.

_____

_____

_____

_____

_____

_____

_____

_____

Life will never give you a challenge without also providing you with all the resources you

_____

_____

_____

_____

_____

_____

_____

_____

_____

_____

_____

need to handle it. Look closely. There is always a way—over, under, around, or through.

MAKE A PROMISE TO YOURSELF.
Keep it.

Never turn your back on your own ideas. The next time you say to yourself, "Hey, that gives

_____

_____

_____

_____

_____

_____

_____

_____

me an idea," add it to your list. Then follow through on each idea to its logical conclusion.

_____

_____

_____

_____

_____

_____

_____

_____

_____

_____

_____

_____

Notice that the most fascinating people are in the habit of talking about what they are *for*, rather than what they are *against*. Their optimism attracts support and propels them forward.

_____

_____

_____

_____

_____

_____

_____

_____

_____

Our lives become so different when we finally decide what's truly important—decide to do

_____

_____

_____

_____

_____

_____

_____

_____

_____

_____

_____

_____

whatever it takes and then start spending our precious time on those things that really matter.

Never give up trying to do whatever you believe to be beautiful and good—whatever you feel is the real you. Always be willing to give up whatever is *preventing* you from doing it.

_____

_____

_____

_____

_____

_____

_____

_____

_____

Intention and commitment are an unbeatable combination. Intention is deciding what you

_____

_____

_____

_____

_____

_____

_____

_____

_____

_____

_____

really want. Commitment is resolving to do whatever it takes to make that **int**ention a reality.

_____

_____

_____

_____

_____

_____

_____

_____

_____

Make your goals manageable. For each yearly goal, create monthly objectives. For each

_____

_____

_____

_____

_____

_____

_____

_____

_____

_____

_____

_____

_____

monthly goal, create weekly objectives. For each weekly goal, create daily objectives.

FIND YOUR HAPPY.

Try this "shortcut to happiness": Make a list of what bugs you about your life and then turn

_____

_____

_____

_____

_____

_____

_____

_____

_____

_____

those negatives into positives. Example: "I really hate my job." Solution: "Find a job I love!"

_____

_____

_____

_____

_____

_____

_____

_____

_____

_____

_____

_____

_____

_____

_____

_____

_____

_____

_____

_____

_____

_____

If your hopes become reality, it will be because of one very special day in your journey:

_____

_____

_____

_____

_____

_____

_____

_____

_____

_____

_____

_____

_____

_____

_____

_____

_____

_____

_____

_____

the day you actually give yourself permission to do what you've always dreamed of doing.

_____

_____

_____

_____

_____

_____

_____

_____

_____

_____

_____

Look forward with high expectations. The future is not something to fear; it's something to anticipate. The future is waiting with open arms. Whatever you're ready for is ready for you.

Use this interactive journal on its own or with the companion book,
10: What's on your top 10 list?

Discover all of the Life by the Numbers books and journals!

5: Where will you be five years
from today?

1: How many people does it take
to make a difference?

2: How will you create something
beautiful together?

7: How many days of the week
can be extraordinary?